The Johnstown Flood

by Marc Tyler Nobleman

Content Adviser: Gregory Zaborowski,
Historian and Education Specialist,
Johnstown Flood National Memorial

Reading Adviser: Rosemary G. Palmer, Ph.D.,
Department of Literacy, College of Education,
Boise State University

COMPASS POINT BOOKS

MINNEAPOLIS, MINNESOTA

Compass Point Books
3109 West 50th Street, #115
Minneapolis, MN 55410

Visit Compass Point Books on the Internet at *www.compasspointbooks.com*
or e-mail your request to *custserv@compasspointbooks.com*

On the cover: Colored lithograph of the devastating Johnstown Flood

Photographs ©: Bettmann/Corbis, cover; Prints Old & Rare, back cover (far left); Library of Congress, back cover, 10, 12, 13, 29, 31, 32, 34; The Granger Collection, New York, 5; Corbis, 7, 36; Johnstown Flood Museum, 8, 11, 15, 17, 21, 22, 25, 27, 38, 40; Nathan Farb/Time Life Pictures/Getty Images, 19; North Wind Picture Archives, 26, 28, 33, 35, 37; Stock Montage, 39.

Managing Editor: Catherine Neitge
Photo Researcher: Svetlana Zhurkin
Designer/Page Production: Bradfordesign, Inc./The Design Lab
Cartographer: XNR Productions, Inc.
Educational Consultant: Diane Smolinski
Library Consultant: Kathleen Baxter

Creative Director: Keith Griffin
Editorial Director: Carol Jones

Library of Congress Cataloging-in-Publication Data
Nobleman, Marc Tyler.
  The Johnstown Flood / by Marc Tyler Nobleman.
      p. cm. — (We the people)
  Includes bibliographical references and index.
  ISBN 0-7565-1267-0 (hardcover)
  1. Floods—Pennsylvania—Johnstown—History—19th century—Juvenile literature. 2. Johnstown (Pa.)—History—19th century—Juvenile literature. I. Title. II. Series: We the people (Series) (Compass Point Books)
  F159.J7N63 2006
  974.8'77—dc22   2005002466

TABLE OF CONTENTS

RESCUED FROM THE RAMPAGE

Heavy rain pounded Johnstown, Pennsylvania, one of the leading steelmaking centers in the United States. The following morning, May 31, 1889, the massive lake behind an old dam in the mountains above Johnstown was bulging with water.

What the townspeople didn't know was that the dam would not hold for much longer and a catastrophe was about to forever change the town.

The rain had turned the front yard of 6-year-old Gertrude Quinn's house into a small pond. She was watching ducks swim in it. Moments later, everyone heard a deafening roar.

A gigantic wall of water barreled down the mountain and into Johnstown, swallowing everything in its path. The dam had burst, and the flood it unleashed plowed into Gertrude's big brick house and whisked it away. Gertrude, her aunt, her baby cousin, and the baby's

An agonized mother watches as her husband and child are swept away in the flood.

nursemaid were still in it. The rest of her family was away or made it safely to high ground.

Of the four left in the house, only Gertrude survived. Just before the house was completely ripped apart, she leapt to a mud-stained mattress drifting by. As the water gushed through town, Gertrude saw destruction all around her. She thought she would die.

A roof with about 20 people clinging to it floated near Gertrude. One of them was Maxwell McAchren, who spotted Gertrude on her makeshift raft.

Although others on the roof warned Maxwell not to try it, he was determined to save Gertrude. He jumped into the water, which may have been as deep as 20 feet (6 meters). His head bobbed under the surface. But every time he came up, he was closer to Gertrude's raft. He was swimming toward her through the mad torrent.

Finally, he got to the girl and climbed onto the mattress. They approached a building that had been spared by the flood. Two men were dangling out a window,

All six people in this house survived the flood.

pulling people from the water. One yelled to McAchren, "Throw that baby to us!"

"Do you think you can catch her?" McAchren yelled back.

"We can try!"

McAchren tossed Gertrude high through the air. She

7

Flood victims grabbed onto whatever they could in hopes of survival.

landed in the arms of one of the men. Gertrude was saved—again. McAchren would also make it through the ordeal, as would Gertrude's parents and siblings.

However, more than 2,200 others in Johnstown that day were not so fortunate.

8

TOWN DESTINED FOR TRAGEDY

Johnstown was founded in 1794 in a valley of the Allegheny Mountains about 70 miles (112 kilometers) east of Pittsburgh. Throughout the century, immigrants from Germany and Wales settled there. By the 1870s, Johnstown was becoming one of the most successful steel manufacturing towns in the country. Its mills produced steel for many things, ranging from common nails to warships. In 1889, the population of Johnstown was 10,000, but 20,000 more people lived in smaller communities nearby.

The town had been built between the Little Conemaugh and Stonycreek rivers. These two rivers joined to form the Conemaugh River. With water surrounding the town, Johnstown's residents became used to minor flooding at least once a year. During storms, the rivers often overflowed onto their banks and

9

The Cambria Iron Works in Johnstown was one of the largest producers of rails.

into the streets of Johnstown. People considered this a
nuisance but nothing more.

Two main factors contributed to this flooding, and
humans caused both of them. First, the settlers had cut

10

down many trees on the slopes of the mountains overlooking the town. This increased the runoff from the rains, which swelled the rivers. Second, settlers needed more room to expand the town, so they filled in part of the rivers with land. That forced the water to flow into a narrower channel.

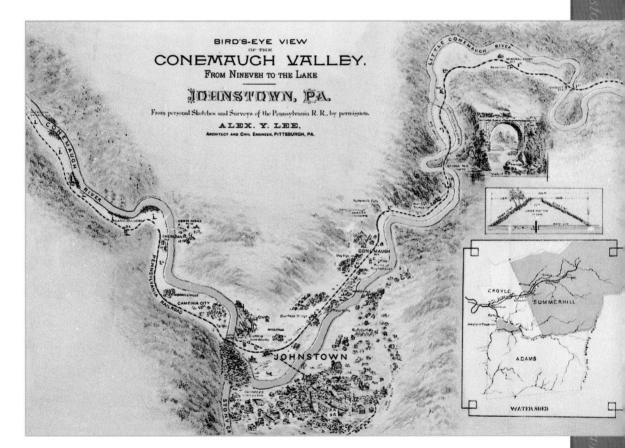

An 1880s map of the Johnstown area

11

Canals, such as the canal at Johnstown, were an important means of transportation.

However, the rivers did not pose the only—or the most dangerous—flooding threat. In 1839, Pennsylvania began building a dam 14 miles (22.4 km) upstream from Johnstown on the Little Conemaugh River. The dam created a reservoir to provide water in dry months for a canal that ran between Johnstown and Pittsburgh. Dam construction took much longer than expected, ending 14 years later. By that time, railroads had overtaken canal boats as the dominant form of transportation. Therefore, the reservoir—which was one of the largest artificial lakes in the nation at the time— and the dam were obsolete even before they were finished.

In 1862, the dam broke. The water drained out of the reservoir but caused little damage to the surrounding property since the lake was only half full.

The dam and the nearly empty reservoir were left to deteriorate until 1879, when the South Fork Fishing and Hunting Club bought the property. This group of wealthy businessmen wanted to turn the area into a private resort. Among its members were Andrew Carnegie and Henry Clay Frick.

Andrew Carnegie was a wealthy industrialist.

The dam was weak and needed repair. It was made of earth, not stone. The club ordered repairs, which took two years, and were carried out without the help of an engineer. As a result, the dam was not adequately improved. Rather than strengthen the dam with masonry, the workers added mud, hay, tree stumps, and other available material.

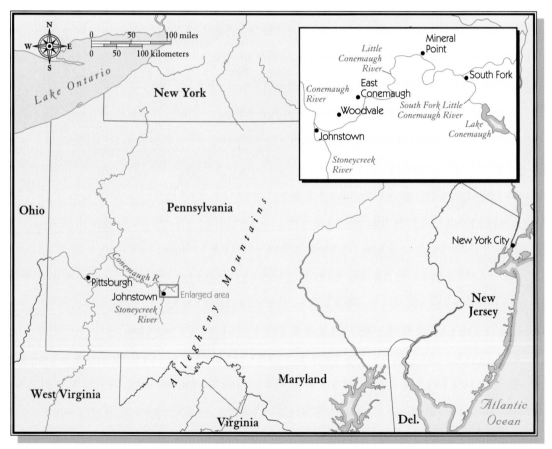

The Little Conemaugh and Stonycreek rivers joined to form the Conemaugh River.

One of 16 cottages on the banks of Lake Conemaugh

Also, they did not replace discharge pipes that had been removed before the club bought the property. This meant there was no way to reduce water in the lake in case of an emergency.

The club had the reservoir refilled with water, called it Lake Conemaugh, and stocked it with 1,000 black bass for fishing. To keep the fish in the lake, the club installed iron bars across the overflow spillway, a part of a dam that allows excess water to flow out. Members also enjoyed hunting and boating on the lake. The club built a 47-room clubhouse at the lake's edge, and some members built luxurious cottages there.

For the next eight summers, club members enjoyed their paradise, and the people in Johnstown went about their daily lives. For some of them, that included predicting if the dam would ever collapse. In 1889, the dam did break again—only this time, the lake was filled to capacity when it happened.

TWENTY MILLION TONS OF WATER

Lake Conemaugh was enormous. It stretched approximately 3 miles (4.8 km) long, 1 mile (1.6 km) wide at its widest spot, and more than 60 feet (18.3 m)

A woodcut of Lake Conemaugh and the huge dam with its spillway

17

deep. It covered 450 acres (180 hectares) and held 20 million tons of water. The dam holding it in was more than 900 feet (274.5 m) long and 72 feet (22 m) high. That is about as wide as three football fields and as high as a seven-story building.

Every spring, when snow melted and rain fell more frequently, Johnstown residents again wondered if the dam could fail. Years passed and the dam held, so people became less fearful. Plus many people in Johnstown assumed that the men who ran the club on the hill would not let anything harm their scenic getaway.

Others, however, were aware that the South Fork Fishing and Hunting Club did not take proper care of the dam. That did not always mean they were worried. After all, Lake Conemaugh was 14 miles (22.4 km) from Johnstown. While some in Johnstown did suspect that the water was capable of reaching their town, not many could imagine the devastation it could do.

A South Fork summer cottage stands unoccupied more than 115 years after the Johnstown Flood.   **19**

DEATH OF A DAM

On Memorial Day 1889, a severe storm began to drench Johnstown and the vicinity. Rain continued through the night. The water level of Lake Conemaugh rose dangerously high. Tree branches and leaves clogged the iron bars over the dam spillway and blocked water from draining. Similarly, there were no discharge pipes to let out water.

The next day, Friday, May 31, was dark and chilly. In the morning, John Parke Jr., the engineer of the South Fork Fishing and Hunting Club, found that the water in the lake was just 4 feet (1.2 m) from the top of the dam— and rising at a rate of 6 inches (15 centimeters) an hour.

Desperate to avoid an accident, Colonel Elias Unger, president of the club, asked laborers to try to fix the problem. In the heavy rain, they attempted to take out the heavy bars in the spillway, dig a new spillway, cut a sluiceway to let out water, and add height to the dam. But none of it worked. Unger realized that he would not be

Lake Conemaugh and the dam can be seen behind club president Elias Unger's house.

able to save the dam, but he could try to save people.

At 11:30 A.M., Unger sent Parke on horseback to warn the people of South Fork, a town 2 miles (3.2 km) below the dam.

Unger also arranged for telegrams to be sent to towns further down the valley, including Johnstown,

El. of Breast of Dam +1618'

72 Ft.

The line at the top of this image of the ruins of the flood shows where the dam had been.

warning them of possible danger. Around noon,

Johnstown received a telegraph message that read:

South Fork Dam is liable to break.

Notify the people of Johnstown to prepare for the worst.

At 1:52 P.M., another message reported that the dam

was overflowing. At 2:45 P.M., a third message warned that

the dam would go any minute. Unger returned to his home north of the dam.

In Johnstown, many residents were underestimating the alarming messages. Some simply ignored them. They had heard too many flood warnings that turned out to be false alarms. Others reacted, but not cautiously enough. Instead of fleeing, residents and business owners moved their belongings from the ground floor to the upper floors to keep them from getting soaked. Then they stayed inside to wait it out. They thought those who left for higher ground were overreacting.

The dam was leaking. Water ran over the top and sliced a notch 10 feet (3 m) wide in it. Then the middle of the dam caved in from the pressure.

At 3:10 P.M., the dam, as one horrified witness described, "just moved away."

THE LAKE ESCAPES

With a thunderous boom, the lake exploded through the dam. The water began hurtling down the winding river valley. It reached speeds of up to 40 miles (64 km) an hour. The force of the water was immense. It tore up everything in its way. It grew to be a grinding, foaming avalanche of yellow-brown water filled with trees, houses, telephone and telegraph poles, mills, bridges, and animals and people, alive and dead.

Locomotives weighing 50 tons were snatched up as if they were leaves. A cloud of black dust swirled around the writhing mass. At its highest point, the wall of water was 89 feet (27 m) high, with an average height of 40 feet (12 m) and a width of half a mile (0.8 km).

Johnstown was not the first community the flood descended upon. One doomed town after another lay ahead of it along the river valley. When the water rolled over South Fork, it killed four people and destroyed up to 30 homes.

24

Next it crashed into Mineral Point, where 16 people died. The main street of this sawmill town was wiped out.

In the critical minutes before the wave rushed into the town of East Conemaugh, a train engineer named John Hess heard a sound "like a hurricane." He frantically tried to warn

The wreckage of the Day Express *passenger train*

The floodwater snatched houses and everything else in its path.

the residents. He rigged his train whistle so it would produce a steady shriek, then he raced to town, rounded up his family, and bolted to the hills. His alert saved many, but 50 people in East Conemaugh were killed.

Between East Conemaugh and the next town, Woodvale, the river valley straightened out, allowing the flood to gather speed. The people of Woodvale had not been warned. Nearly one-third of the residents died, 314 out of 1,100. Only a mill was left standing. When the Gautier Wire Works was destroyed, its boilers blew up and created what

witnesses called a black "death mist." Gautier made barbed
wire, which was sucked into the water.

In only 45 minutes, the entire lake had emptied down
the mountain. A menacing wind blew into Johnstown before
the water appeared. Many heard a roar before they saw the
cause of it. By the time the flood rumbled in, it contained so
much debris from the previous towns that some people said

In the small town of Woodvale, 250 houses were destroyed.

27

A view of the broken dam as seen from inside the reservoir appeared in Harper's Weekly.

they could barely see the water. It covered the town at 4:07 P.M.,
57 minutes after the dam gave out. In some places, the water
was three stories high.

28

Then the floodwaters split, leaving some buildings in the center of town unharmed. The northern section of town was hit the hardest. Wooden houses splintered or were swept up whole. Brick houses crumbled. One person said the flood "crushed houses like eggshells." One woman's house was hit by a locomotive. From his office, one man counted 63 bodies that floated by in 20 minutes.

Up ahead where the two rivers met stood a stone bridge built by the Pennsylvania Railroad. The end of the flood was near, but not the end of the misery.

The center of Johnstown escaped the flood's destruction.

29

PILE-UP AT THE STONE BRIDGE

Even with multiple flood warnings, some residents of Johnstown were still caught by surprise. Since the rivers surrounding the town had spilled onto land, parts of the town were already under several feet of water. That made last-minute escape difficult. Some people did not even try. They huddled in attics and hoped the flood would miss them.

People suffered in many ways. Some ran for safety and got separated from their families. Some drowned. Some who were thrown from buildings into the water managed to pull themselves onto a piece of floating debris, often a dislodged roof. Some were pinned between chunks of debris or snagged in barbed wire. Some were pushed to the place that would ultimately stop the flood—the Pennsylvania Railroad Company's old stone bridge at the junction of the Little Conemaugh and the Stonycreek rivers.

The Johnstown Flood was over in 10 minutes.

Though the bridge was the only obstacle in 14 miles (22.4 km) that withstood the flood, it soon turned into a horrible scene. Hurled by the water, thousands of tons of wreckage slammed into the bridge, one jagged piece after another, piling up 40 feet (12 m) high. It included entire houses, freight cars, train tracks, machinery, uprooted trees, livestock, and dead bodies. Live victims trapped in the twisted

The pile of debris at the stone bridge covered 30 acres (12 hectares).

31

Many people who survived the flood died in the fire at the bridge.

mess screamed and struggled for a way out. Some who got free tried to help others.

Near nightfall, oil from a railroad car caught fire and created an inferno. By several estimates, 300 people who had survived the flood did not survive the flames. The fire blazed for three days.

RELIEF AND RECOVERY

Johnstown was in shambles. By 6 P.M., the town could not communicate with the outside world because the flood toppled telegraph poles. The outside world, however, came to Johnstown. Two groups—reporters and aid workers— were first on the scene.

More than 100 newspapers and magazines sent writers to the town, some of whom traveled the final miles on foot.

Four square miles (10.4 square kilometers) of downtown Johnstown were destroyed.

33

Johnstown's Main Street was destroyed.

This was an era before news photography was widespread, so the publications sent illustrators, too. This was also an era when reporters often exaggerated or outright lied about the details. Before newspapers had accurate figures, some printed that half of the population of Johnstown had been killed.

The actual number of dead was lower but heartbreaking just the same. The death toll was 2,209. That included more than 750 people who could not be identified. Many more were injured. Ninety-nine entire families perished, including 396 children. Some bodies were never found, while others were discovered miles away and even years later. After the flood, typhoid fever spread, killing at least 40 more.

Approximately 1,600 homes and 280 businesses were destroyed. Property damage was $17 million, which would be more than $300 million in today's currency.

That night, emergency hospitals and morgues were set up. Some survivors stayed in the few buildings left intact. Others who were now home- less clustered together on the dark hillsides. By the time the sun rose, the water had receded. Filthy rubble lay in heaps three stories tall. Bodies were every- where. After a day of unbear-

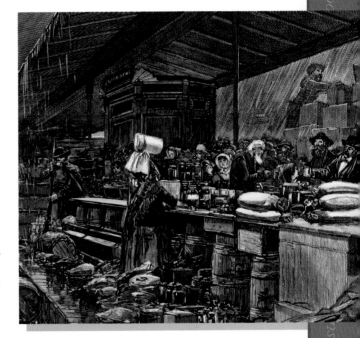

A relief station and morgue were set up at the train depot.

35

able noise, there was now silence. It looked as though Johnstown had been scraped off the face of the planet.

Johnstown did not have to bear the burden of recovery alone. Though the federal government did not yet provide disaster relief funds, people from every state sent some type of aid. Pennsylvania prisoners sent bread. Residents of Cincinnati, Ohio, sent ham. People from Detroit, Michigan, sent chairs. Various groups, including police officers from New York and baseball players from Missouri, sent money. Farmers brought food almost immediately. At least 16 countries including Russia, Turkey, France, Great Britain, Australia, and Germany sent aid as well.

Survivors lived in a shack on the site of their old home.

A Red Cross warehouse was the first building constructed after the flood.

On June 5, Clara Barton and 50 members of a new organization called the American Red Cross arrived to help. Barton stayed until October. The Red Cross built hotels and warehouses to store the supplies that people donated. They handed out food and clothing. At its peak, Johnstown drew 7,000 volunteers.

Despite this outpouring of help, cleanup would take years. But by July 1, 1889, stores began to reopen. People were beginning to heal.

RESPONSIBILITY AND REMEMBRANCE

Outraged residents in Johnstown and people around the country wanted to know who was responsible for the disaster. Some people said the flood was an act of God since humans had no control over the weather. Others disagreed. They blamed the South Fork Fishing and

A Johnstown man blamed the disaster on the South Fork Fishing and Hunting Club. He placed a sign (left) next to the gravestones of his family. It read: Family of X.J. Swank, wife and four children drowned by the South Fork Fishing and Hunting Club. May 31st, 1889.

FRANK LESLIE'S ILLUSTRATED JOHNSTOWN NEWSPAPER

No. 1760.—Vol. LXVIII.]   NEW YORK—FOR THE WEEK ENDING JUNE 8, 1889.   [Price, 10 Cents.

PENNSYLVANIA.—THE APPALLING DISASTER AT JOHNSTOWN—ENORMOUS DESTRUCTION OF LIFE AND PROPERTY BY A FLOOD FROM THE MOUNTAINS.—SCENE BELOW THE DEVASTATED TOWN.—[SEE PAGE 311.]

The front page of Frank Leslie's Illustrated Newspaper *from June 1889*

The library built by Andrew Carnegie now houses the Johnstown Flood Museum.

Hunting Club for not repairing the dam correctly and
not maintaining it regularly. Still others viewed the flood
as a combination of natural and manmade causes.

40

People filed lawsuits against the South Fork Fishing and Hunting Club, but its members were never charged with a crime. They also never apologized for or even commented publicly on the flood. The club soon broke up. Only a few of its members assisted families of survivors. One of them, Andrew Carnegie, paid for the construction of a new library in Johnstown.

The Johnstown Flood was one of the biggest news stories in the United States in the second half of the 19th century. It was also one of the deadliest disasters in American history, both in terms of lives lost and property ruined. The tragedy has been remembered in books, poems, songs, and films.

In 1889, though a dam and a series of towns disintegrated, the spirit of the survivors did not. The people of Johnstown mourned and rebuilt their town at the same time.

Nobody rebuilt the dam.

GLOSSARY

debris—the remains of something broken or destroyed

deteriorate—to become steadily worse

discharge pipes—pipes in a dam that allow water to be released when the water level gets too high

immigrants—people who move from one country to live permanently in another

inferno—an intense fire

masonry—structure built of stone or brick

morgues—places where dead bodies are kept temporarily

obsolete—no longer in use; out-of-date

recede—to move back and away from

reservoir—an artificial lake where water is collected

runoff—rain that is not absorbed by the soil

sluiceway—a passage that allows water to pass over or around a dam; spillway

DID YOU KNOW?

- The Johnstown Flood contained about the same amount of water that goes over Niagara Falls in 36 minutes.

- After the flood, some people in Johnstown lived in a temporary wooden shelter called an Oklahoma house. These early examples of prefabricated buildings were originally developed in Chicago for homesteaders living in the Oklahoma Territory. They were one-and-a-half stories and came in two sizes, 10-by-20 feet (3-by-6 m) and 16-by-24 feet (4.8-by-7.3 m).

- In 1936, another flood in Johnstown killed 25 people, and a flood-control project was started there the following year. But in 1977, the Conemaugh River flooded again and killed 85 people.

- A movie about the Johnstown Flood won the 1990 Academy Award for best short documentary. It is shown hourly at the Johnstown Flood Museum, which commissioned the film to mark the flood's 100th anniversary.

- Andrew Carnegie founded more than 2,500 libraries around the world. The library he built in Johnstown after the flood was one of the first.

IMPORTANT DATES

Timeline

1794	Johnstown, Pennsylvania, is founded.
1839	Pennsylvania begins building a dam and reservoir in the mountains above Johnstown.
1862	The dam breaks for the first time.
1879	The South Fork Fishing and Hunting Club purchases the reservoir and turns it into a pleasure lake.
1889	The dam breaks, spilling 20 million tons of water onto the towns below and causing many deaths.
1936	Johnstown floods again and 25 people die.
1937	A flood-control system is built.
1977	Johnstown floods again and 85 people die.

IMPORTANT PEOPLE

CLARA BARTON (1821–1912)
Nurse who founded the American Red Cross and provided aid to the victims of the Johnstown Flood

ANDREW CARNEGIE (1835–1919)
Wealthy industrialist, member of the South Fork Fishing and Hunting Club, and philanthropist who founded libraries in Johnstown and elsewhere

JOHN HESS (1840–1899)
Train engineer whose heroic actions saved lives in the Pennsylvania town of East Conemaugh on the day of the flood

GERTRUDE QUINN SLATTERY (1883–1974)
Survivor of the Johnstown Flood who wrote a book for her children, Johnstown and Its Flood, *in 1936*

COLONEL ELIAS UNGER (1830–1896)
President of the South Fork Fishing and Hunting Club when the dam broke in 1889

WANT TO KNOW MORE?

At the Library

Dahlstedt, Marden. *The Terrible Wave.* New York: Coward, McCann & Geoghegan, 1972.

Gallagher, Jim. *The Johnstown Flood.* Philadelphia: Chelsea House Publications, 2000.

Gow, Mary. *Johnstown Flood: The Day the Dam Burst.* Berkeley Heights, N.J.: Enslow Publishers, 2003.

Gross, Virginia. *The Day It Rained Forever: A Story of the Johnstown Flood.* New York: Puffin, 1993.

Walker, Paul Robert. *Head for the Hills (Read It to Believe It!).* New York: Random House, 1993.

On the Web

For more information on the *Johnstown Flood,* use FactHound
to track down Web sites related to this book.

1. Go to *www.facthound.com*

2. Type in a search word related to this book
   or this book ID: 0756512670

3. Click on the *Fetch It* button.

Your trusty FactHound will fetch the best Web sites for you!

On the Road

Johnstown Flood Museum

301 Washington St.

Johnstown, PA 15901

888/222-1889

To learn more about the Johnstown

Flood and its aftermath

Johnstown Flood National Memorial

733 Lake Road

South Fork, PA 15956

814/495-4643

To view the remains of the South

Fork Dam and see an award-winning

film about the flood

Look for more We the People books about this era:

Angel Island

The Great Chicago Fire

Great Women of the

　Suffrage Movement

The Harlem Renaissance

The Haymarket Square Tragedy

The Hindenburg

Industrial America

The Lowell Mill Girls

Roosevelt's Rough Riders

A complete list of We the People titles is available on our Web site:
www.compasspointbooks.com

INDEX

About the Author

Marc Tyler Nobleman is the author of more than 40 books for young people. He writes regularly for *Nickelodeon Magazine* and has written for The History Channel. He is also a cartoonist whose single panels have appeared in more than 100 international publications, including the *Wall Street Journal, Good Housekeeping,* and *Forbes.* He lives with his wife and daughter in Connecticut.